© 2018 by Dawn Renee.   All rights reserved.
Published by Vantage Point Publishing
Indianapolis, IN 46205

No part of this publication may be reproduced or transmitted in any form or by any means, electronic or mechanical, including photocopy, or any information storage and retrieval system, without permission from the publisher. The only exception is a brief quotation in printed reviews.

Limit of Liability/Disclaimer of Warranty: While the publisher and author have used their best efforts in preparing this book, they make no representations or warranties with respect to the accuracy or completeness of the contents of this book and specifically disclaim any implied warranties of merchantability or facilities for a particular purpose. No warranty may be created or extended by any persons. The advice or strategies herein may not be suitable for your situation. You should consult with a professional where appropriate. Neither the publisher nor author should be liable for any loss of profit or any other incidental damages, including but not limited to special, consequential, or other damages.

This is a work of fiction. Names, characters, businesses, places, events and incidents are either the products of the author's imagination or used in a fictitious manner. Any resemblance to actual persons, living or dead, or actual events is purely coincidental.

ISBN **978-1-943159-09-3**

LCCN 2018949276

The publisher would appreciate notification where errors occur so that they may be corrected in subsequent printing and/or editions. Please send comments to the publisher by emailing to deeprivers67@yahoo.com

Printed in the United States of America

Ink Stains

by

Dawn Renee

Manipulated to believe

As the walls slowly come down

The heat starts to build

I sit and listen to your lies

I sit and listen to a story that has been told so many times

The letters don't even respond

Words lost

Searching for understand with the ability to

If only you told the truth

I reach the conclusion that you don't know what truth is

Your lies form quicker

Than the truth can be told

Believing what you say

Convincing no one but your self

That the lies you spit

Is nothing but falsehoods of who you are!

Entertained long enough for you to hang

Yourself

My mind speaks for itself

Walks strong in building of a foundation

That you will never tear down

Your loss

Your loss

Your bullshit

That only you

Believe

Can you conceive truth?

Not with me

But self

As long as you continue to lie to you

You will be the only one that listens to you

Lies of selfishness

Makes for a lonely heart….

My words have fallen on empty reasons

Lips caressed while the tears fall

And the understanding of what

Has taken a turn for a different path

To see what holds me

Protects me from fear

The light the shines temporary

At falsehoods that visit my doorstep

I see with closed eyes

And hear through loud screams

The twisting of emotions

That cages my soul

As my spirit

Whispers

I love you…..

When love seems to just walk on by

and passes me in the process

I am not foreign to what love has to offer

or am I?

The constant question that never seems to

have the same answer

Wishful thoughts of what will be

in time

No rush for the wrong kiss

but the kiss that is meant just for me

placed

at

the

right

time

right

place

so I

wait.....

"Recquisitions of Mind and Body,......Soul to be Cont......."

He words slipped inside of my thoughts

Whispers became screams

of what I wanted

and what he was willing to give

and at that moment

I realized

that I

possessed the power

to obtain my pleasure

not what someone could give

but what I needed to give me

first

He smiled and said with a voice

that sent chills beyond me

That I could have all that he had to offer

And I replied

Kiss me until my pain smiles back....

The mood of the sun
warm and understanding
when the moon hides waiting
for the right time to reveal itself
night is my place of calm
energy high
and flow
seems
to
take over
giving me a burst of fire
to need
want
desires
soar
and the sweet smell of mangoes
and fresh honey escape
the valley of fear
no longer exist
as cravings
skip my heart beat
my addictions
with knowing
what

is
to
be......

My words are my pathway to my soul...

expressing never imagined...

real as the ink that pours....

the paper that receives my solemn story....

words that lift me...

but only if they would catch me....

the reality that sits...

deep...

the rivers that overflow with tears of a heart half full....

discarded upon the waters...

with hopes that they drift back this way....

my words are my story....

pen the direction...

the paper in which the flow will go....

to write on paper...

does it disappear with each stroke written....

and then the moment comes...

and all is still...

as the next move spills from my pen....

to know me is to venture into a world of many pieces of blank

pages...

words that stay only for the moment...

with the hope of staying for a lifetime.......

Whispering through the mind

Of a woman

She is more than the heat she can create

More than most ever seem to see

She is so many things

And the list continues with the birth of every

Baby girl

Standing at the cross roads of life

And I realize that we must

Know our own worth

Never selling ourselves less

Caress yourself

Love yourself

Protect yourself

First

And then those around

Can only see the light

The armor of love that you carry

A heart spilled gold

Molded each day

Your eyes open

To another day

Of challenges

That you can take head on

Whisper to yourself

I love you

More and more

Each time I look in your eyes

Whisper freedom

Into

You

Hearts mended

Lives spent

On building

You

See as I look in the mirror

What I despised and was told was wrong

I had to fall over and over

Again

In

Love

With

Me…….

Very loud, decibel piercing. ...."The Resounding Stare"

As the sun disappears....

and the darkness of night rests in my soul....

you hear the whispers of my mind....

replaced with the screams that you see...

the calm that resonates in my spirit of dreams ....

so it seems...

as I tilt my head just enough to gaze into the eyes...

that read my soul...

lips that speak to my spirit....

caressing my body with your thoughts ....

the energy electrifying....

with no words ever spoken....

as you shift gears in my dreams ....

the outcome foreseen ...

as the rivers of our souls enter into ecstasy....

He says I do

You say I do

As we become one

We do

The beauty of the wedding

Love in the air

Now that the easy part has been done

The work begins

Desire to stay married

Never a fad

The life of $1+1=1$

As we walk hand in hand

I am your Queen

Standing beside, in front and behind you

To always be there

As you my King

The provider, protector

Being the head of our household

We are one as we walk this path of love

God first, as he is the head, the light and the way

My husband second, he is my all

I am his wife, lover, friend and confidant

Together we provide a home of comfort and peace

For our family to be

In God's Covenant of life

"A Kindred Spirit's Journey,.......The recognition of My Soul

He brought tears to my eyes

I walked the path of nowhere

When I reached the crossroad of life

The vision seem to come so strong

From the shining sun

That beamed its light upon me

The direction that pulls at me

The desire

That consumes me

Deep in my soul

Longing for his touch

Just once

If not forever

See the ability to know

Who I am

What I desire

My deepest needs

The yearning

That reaches my inner sanctity

And yet stands still

The beast that wants to devour you

Waiting for the moment

To release

The sun upon caramel kissed eyes

With a burning red heart

For the addiction that contemplates

Manipulating my mind

Into what can't be

But I still stand in my purpose

Of loving harder than steel

I am love

Whispering

Moaning

Screaming

I am addicted…..

I submit....

to what protects the heart....

continues to keep the fire burning.....

vested in more than mere holdings.....

invest in my life line. ....

more than a passing through time.....

longevity. ....

my passion creates many paths of fury....

desires that no longer will be manipulated....

constant needing to feel conquered....

as I prefer chocolate. ....

never acquired.....

the taste of vanilla. ....

as wet as the rain that falls outside...

my window. ....

the desires needs to fall from.....

my inner walls......summer rain upon us once again

A creature so fragile....

but...

so strong in many ways....

how does she pass the moment...

and walk in the light of purpose....

my mind is gifted...

this she knows...

but needing direction...

thou shall not waste....

accomplished of...

captured by...

wanting more than just existing...

a mere passing in the night....

my destiny...

closer than the taste on my lips...

that slips...

with confusion...

delusion...

that I know is there....

I want what is mine....

and nothing less....

my inner sanctity....

disturbed...

with so many battles...

so many wants...

needs...

desires...

wants that trap....

needs to break free...

and desires that feed my addiction...

accomplishment ?.....in search of

I slipped into me

The lyrically engineered voice

That has more to say than those to listen

I dived deep into me

And at that moment I realize

That who I thought I was

And who others thought me to be

Was never in existence

I am the lost voice

That passion that screams to the mountain tops

And floods the valley with

Sweet honey and mango nectar

I will give my last breath to see

The smile that I wiped across your face

See

The reality is

You thought

And that was the first mistake

You wanted the moon and stars

And got darkness

How does one propose to another and then walk away

How does he propose and he has yet to touch her

And then he pit the proposal

On the table

And silence

Came

As he has not a clue

That she loves deep than any vessel can dive

Into the deep blue sea

And her heart is that of forever love

She gives deep and just wants the same passion in return

And you say you love her

Is it possible to love someone?

That is the moon and the stars but you keep them hidden

Behind the clouds

I wanted and discovered the tears falling

And at that moment

I asked the question

Do you really know what love is?

The commitment that accompanies love

Do you have a clue?

Most never do…..

Sitting in darkness

As the music plays to my soul

I drift to a place of peace

Where my mind felt free

And my body opened the closed walls

I slipped and let him in

Yes he came so far in

That my breathing was at his command

I never knew

What freedom

Unadulterated freedom

Felt

Like

And

At this moment

The shackles released

The lips spoke

With a sense of righteousness

See I floated above the past

And landed on an island of mine

My thoughts

My addictions

My wants and desires

Insatiable

Appetite that wanted to inhale

His consciousness

I needed to adapt my dreams to reality

And labor the pains into now

Continuous music he plays

Strung up and out

As the bass

Created a new melody for my heart

My thighs reverted back to my days of the splits and all night dancing

I slipped and he gave

Me

What was stripped so many years ago

My freedom to breath……

Will you caress me?

Correct the loneliness I feel

Blanket me in warmth

As you protect me from my fears

That creeps into my dreams

Holding me close

Be the peace to my storm

As I confess

I don't want to sleep alone

Anymore…..

The many reasons the sun rises

The same ones apply to the setting of the same

The waterfalls continue to be just as beautiful

As the raindrops that fall

Creating a rainbow in the sky

My eyes are lifted

With hopes of the same beauty to fall upon

A soul that forever believes in love…..

Deep, uninevitable, hope lost, fantasy unfound, slain dreams, given all, still not to be............."The Regrets of Unmirrored Love"

She realized
The hard way
That his head was oversized
Causing his heart to be paralyzed
To the love that stood before his eyes
And he walked away
He shut down his reality
His past hurt was a tragedy
And convinced himself that he was okay
The problem
She loved him anyway
Through it all she knew he would walk at some point
She loved him anyway
Friends knew she was going through
But what no one really knew
The pain that grew
Over many years of past hurt
She loved him anyway
Or did she fall in love with the thought of love
Not knowing what real love really was
When you don't get what you want

And don't want what you have
Does that have anything to do with love?
The thin line that sits between
Wants and needs
That defines the thoughts one goes through
Can you walk away with nothing?
And still feel complete
Or is that a feeling of defeat
She loved him
He only loved himself
Or did he?
Reality
They both were all alone……

I need to feel what it feels like without emptiness

To see the stars at night without the disarray of darkness

See what was at one time

Has never been for me

Perception of reality that lives in a fantasy

And misunderstands what lies before her

She is beyond the capabilities of not loving

But love never loves her back

The discernment

Gives me

Nothing

The heart of opportunity

That rises and crashes with each fix

She is more than an occasional

Breath

Occasional

Stroke of passion

It is so much more to the complexity

Of her

She is

The light that never shines

But shines all the same

Blinding what never arrives

To the destination of humility

That boils deep inside her

She is the struggle of reparations

The fight to survive in a world that checked her, a loss cause

From birth

Strength built on a foundation that she reaches for

The next brick to continue building

Eyes the glare into your soul and you have no clue

Who she is

What she represents

The value of her worth

The diamond never polished

But still more valuable than what is shown

Because your thought has always been

What she is not

And she

The addict

That craves

What he will know

And fulfill

Because he will know the real her

Without her voice being heard

She is

Love…..

When your mind and body go into battle

The lust of my flesh

More than a commonality

Deep rooted in my soul

Fucking that I know can't stop until all the pain is gone

While my mind just wants to be loved like the little girl

That begs to be

I am exhausted with what should be

And trapped in what never comes to pass

The reality is I am in solitude

Fighting a battle all alone

Thoughts washed up on the beach of despair

My voice not heard

My screams turned into silence

My orgasms fight to be released

While I gasp for breath

This battle of mind over matter

And the reality is what matters

Steps taken

Dragged back to the starting gate

And I stand still waiting for the gun to fire

To once again attempt to be

And each time

The red light

Stuck

Never turning green

I walk in darkness

Not running as I am not afraid

Because my life

Consists of dark

Shades of hell

A warrior that never stands down

But realizes the comfort of being in despair

More than the opposite

I am a soul that fights to give up

With a heart that refuses

My battle

To fight…..

Many deposits made into my soul

Enriched with passion and erotic flavors

He gave what was needed

Craved

Created from countless strokes of want

As with each deposit

The fire grew

With the additive of filth that left his lips

Directed at me that caused the flow to burst at the valve of release

And wash upon his soul

Deposits thick and creamy

While his lips

Captured the spirit

That battled with him to see who's desire was stronger

See what he gave

I took

And what I gave he chained around his neck

As the medal of pleasure

Breast full of pain

Waiting to be milked

While fresh plums firm and ripe

Swinging from his vine thick and erect

Waited to be licked and sucked

Until plump was no longer

Many deposits made into my soul

Caused my addiction

To break free like the beast

That was captured with his tongue

And with the slightest movement

I crawl to him to please…..

I need to feel again

Hope to love one more time

Never had it

But I know it was

Somewhere deep inside you

I have to believe

That when the wind blows

You are near

The rain drops are your tears

That kisses my tears

Longing for you

I need to feel again

As my body numb to all reality

Lost upon the horizon

In search of

What I never had

But I know resided in you

Each word I write

The brushstrokes of my

The heart that cries

While my mind deciphers

What was never for me?

But I know it resides somewhere in you

I wish I knew

Could feel

Once

But I never will

The broken pieces of my soul

Held together

By the strings of the unraveled warmth

That never touches my cold wanting hand

I will never know

Understand the

Walking with the shadows

I will never know a mother's love…..

Silence

Soft whispers

Intoxicating aroma

Thoughts go many ways

Lost in the mirage of what the vision creates

I needed to see

Feel

Inhale

Taste

All that he is

My mind playing tricks

Flooded desires run deep

Heat rises

Juices flow

And still I wait

For

The

Moment

To have him

The voice of reason slips into the darkness

While his voice floats above me

Infiltrating my minds eyes

Complete disregard for right

As my needs are those of a beast

Prowling

Hungry

He is my fix

As I am his addiction....

The vision of one's being, inner, outer, the question of heart, mind and soul, the state of discovery..........."The Fright of Self Worth"

Fear consumes me
Doubt seems to slip into my thoughts
My reality is beyond the clouds
I see through the shadows of knowing
Blurred lines that cross the sky
Confusion with slates of delusion
The intrusion
That complicates the growth
Stagnant in a mirage of conclusions
Eclectic functionality
Freedom comes at a price
Willing to sacrifice
To be the black rose
That grows in darkness
And shines in light
Fear consumes me
As I fear me…..

Kiss me with your eyes

As the darkness inside me fades into my shadow

My pain blended into many colors of forgotten dreams

See I realized that what is or was

Never has been

Used and discarded along the path going to a place of nowhere

I am so much more than that

And I simply sit in the valley

Lost in the wilderness of my desires

My voice screams in silence

While my tears wash away with the fallen raindrops

Trapped in a circle of delusion

Suffering more each day

Kiss me with your eyes

To read my pain….

My mind carries me to my home

Heritage rich

Cultural defined

With ancestors that whisper in the winds

I know where my heart is

Destined to be there

Crafted on the backs of Kings

Queens that nurture and raise greatness

When you have no account of who you are

And the lack of purpose for you

My tears are the raindrops that fall

Each one represents a part of me

Eyes see in the darkness that carries such beauty

Shades that are plenty

With features that speak

Who we are

No need to be otherwise

Standing strong with cries of freedom

See I know my spirit won't be settled until I am on my knees

In the rich soil of home

The beginning

Where riches are plenty

Culture is strong and faith long standing

The presence of who I am

African soil

Music that flows to the heart of you

And peace like no other

Home….

I need to feel

Tasting the flavor of you

My mind reminisces about what could be

With a body that craves the reality

Of you

Are my desires unobtainable

Does he exist

To satisfy my addiction

Hard steady strokes

Lips that inhale more than my juices

But between the days of expectancy

Fire that continues to rage

Demanding to be given

The attention of

Pleasing the intricate sensations

Of emotions

That flood the Nile

The beast that sits in the pit of want

In search it's prey

Insatiable appetite

Needs to be fed

I am an addict

Addicted to you.....

I cursed my soul

You sat back and allowed the constant grief to enter

Slapped the image that falls over and over again

See I try hard to understand

To rationalize the ability to continue

The reasons why I love life

Love given

And nothing

Ever comes back in return

My heart shelled in ice

Fighting to release

Fire that rages

While my emotions suffocate themselves

I cursed my soul

Body on fire

Mind is disarray

With a fight that is slowly losing

Its race

See no matter what I continue to go against what I know is the

End of my story

Love fell into the pit of hell

While lust sat back and laughed at what will never be

I am

Who"

I no longer know

Numb to reality

Stuck in a fantasy

With an image stuck in my mind

Happiness that seems to walk sideways

In my world

I let love control what I want the most

To be loved in returned…..

Lay your hand upon my skin
Feel the heat that escapes
The pain that craves you
The pain that temporarily gives me hope
Nothing against my skin
Will alleviate the pain
That runs from head to toe
Nothing releases me from the pain
I
See
Hear and close my eyes to
And it still exists
My pain greater than any thing you can ever
Imagine
When pains controls life
I am
I will
Continue
My purpose His plan.....

My words explode from inside

Cravings that build

Wants and desires that spill onto

A canvas of erotica

Mind filled with fantasy

Words that stroke me into yet another

World of necessity

To fuel my addiction

Your words entice me

I close my eyes and feel your caress

Your lips tour my frame

And your hands sculpt the path

That you will go

Closed eyes

See

With an open mind

Heart filled with passion

To paint life new

My words explode from the inside

With you deep in me

And then I realize

Eyes open

That I am afraid of my

Own words…..

" life of an addict"

The box that has kept me from me
cement structure that holds the tales of my darkness
raped, molested and abused but the smile that appears
never tells the secrets that never releases the light, but you did
you came into my life and started stripping away
what was put there by others not self, but you held
on strong to the darkness and I chipped away
see the ink fueled the pen and the pen beat away at the paper
writing a new beginning to the ending of the hurt and turmoil
that you went through, experienced and lived through
see the once little girl that thought she was thrown out with the
trash
poetry saved her life, one pen stroke, one key stroke, one stone
broke
one voice at a time

I have to admit

the ability to peel the layers

reveal the truth

of what is to be

what was...is

what is...ain't

what would...should

what could....never touched the surface

see the ability to reveal the truth

that lies beneath the reality

that your truth and mine

is the reverse of a just cause

slowly distorted for the picture

when the book was written

with the blood and tears

of justification

without verification

lost in the words of realization

see when you fall in love

you slowly slip into

the passion of danger

never looking for safety

because the intensity

that he brings

gives

the orgasmic smile
from the inside out

I asked, "Can you feel me dreaming of you?"

And silence was the answer

No words spoken or the least utterance of a sound released

I asked again and again silence

Your lips turned away from the hurt in my eyes

And the tears began their journey

Nothing seemed real

I knew what was to be

Or at least my thoughts did

And the calculation was wrong

Many emotions that add up to nothing

So the tears began their journey of restoration

I lost it all

Or for the moment thats how my insides felt

And I stood still

Walking around with the wrong time for the right reasons but the right time for wrong time for confusion to win

See I needed to re evaluate my eyes lips and heart

Put them on the same page in this book of life

And tell myself again

I want to be the priority of your sunrise....

And the warmth of your sunset

See without me believing in me, who would

I had cried a river and the tears still fall

I accepted that
When her love lost all color...Poetry used her tears to paint her a new rainbow

I needed to talk

See what has been going on has to stop

Or is it possible after all these years

Degradation

Manipulation

Condemnation

To name a few

Of the vile mishaps that I have been privy to

Washed in the darkness

When my skin glows in the nights of hell

See I have danced with the devil

And his two step wasn't up to par

Sat him down and his servants just stared at the ease of my style

The reality was is and always will be

That no matter your flavor

Mine is sweeter

Beauty is my enemy that fights my battle for me

As I fear the beast in the mirror

Even though it constantly stares back with a smile that lights the same as the sun

But I

Think I

Should I

And I never do

I needed to talk but silence won the battle

While the eyes in the mirror wait for the war

I need to

Maybe one day I will

Fluid

At times it flows at a steady pace

Other times standing still

As if time ironically stopped

Emotions that fill the half full

Or is it half empty glass

That continues to pour out

With little left

Drops that remain

While nothing is given back

But never empty

Eyes wide shut

While ears listen

Realizing yet again that a refill is needed

A necessity

Or destiny token of admission

Flowing through and out

Falling over the waterfall sides

And even then the ability to refill happens

Overflowing

Constant fluidity

Of the seen and unseen

That which is felt deep beneath what we must

Discover

Allow me to flow now..

My days and nights
The in between hours that flutter
about in the midst of the wicked
While being a wounded butterfly
When love hides and last replaces
In the chair reigning supreme
Heat beyond the fire
Of gesture
But the righteous heir to a throne
That gives only to wait
To receive
Tasting
Licking
Fondling
Caressing
Stimulation
That runs from the outside in
Needing to be taken to heights that
Only addiction knows
The true definition of her desires
She slips into a mirage of how deep
He should go and deep is never
Deep enough
She craves for more each time he

Completes the task of the insatiable appetite
That lays before him
Exhausted and she wants more
To continuously feel him penetrating
To the core of her lava
She is addicted to the sensations
That run from her toes through the eyes of knowing she wants
more
She loves to explodes over and over
Again
Then to explode even more
An emotion that brings the fullness that her soul desires
Orgasms after orgasms
Moans of beauty
When he whispers my name
As he is exhausted with no air left to scream

You are.....

My words, searched under the rocks

over the hilltops and through the fog of cloudy tears

I search for understanding even when I overstand

Yes, my words from my fingertips to the the keyboard to the screen

They appear but in all actuality....they are still not here

My words lost upon the sea of past tears that constantly flow

Your smile, soft sweet and genuine as the diamond picked from the mines

And no matter the situation or circumstance you always smiled and that is how I remember you and will continue to remember

the smile....soft as pure cotton

the eyes....that whisper it is all going to be okay

the hugs....of nothing but unconditional love

and then your words....sultry alluring words

Beautiful words just like the Queen you are....

and we all sit and smile as your words float through the air

and land in the hearts of the ears that listen....

You are...and always will be my friend....until our pens meet again...

Cultivating the hidden wounds

Forward not backwards

Lifted up from the darkness

Of sunlight

Trapped no longer

His words spoke to the moon and traveled back to my soul

He needed what I wanted

Stripped of yesterday's message

Educated in the morning breathe of who she is

Beauty and substance

Submissive to a King

Not fallen by the sword

Crucified by a past gone wrong

But she flourishes in the cement of her destiny

What was...is

A Queen of reality

Loved by her. ...first

Time to go forward with the intensity of life

Can he love what was broken

Wounded in

Tossed out

Mended back

He loves her

Because she loves her self

First

Even when she doesn't see it

Her beauty shines in his eyes

His words whisper life

To be...

Sorry never paid rent
Hasn't experienced life and death
through hours of labor
But constantly resides in the mouths of apologies
The travesty that two words
Become the temporary fix for long term problems
I'm sorry doesn't reside here
So stop allowing it to be a reoccurring
Resident of your life
Send sorry back to the damn chalkboard
And demand substance
Not words with false return

Numb

Nonexistent

Anxiety

Apprehensive

Trapped in a maze of smoke

Reasons beyond understanding that contain information on the sidewalk

Crossing the crossroads

Back stroking in the dark

My mind has been discussed with me

Laughter that was once tears

Draining me of juices

That is why was what

See constantly changing

And remaining the same as the bottom of the top

Beast that boasts

Addiction that's addicted

And the reality is

That I am

A writer

Or am I

A writer

Depends on the definition or who you ask

But my words speak

Of

Emotions

Sailed into nowhere

Broken

The air suffocating on the infusion of hate

Life strangulation

Heavy hearts

Frustration overload

When color causes the senseless deaths

Beauty snatched from the once fresh air

That is now stagnant

Fear that stops a Sunday drive

Frozen walks in the park

A simple step outside ones door

And I ask why

Once again the color of our skin

We see beauty

Not the death sentence

Hate attempts to dish out

We will not be moved

Scared into the night

As the sun will shine upon the lives of the gone too soon

Justice will be served

or am I simply

just a writer with words

I fly with one wing

The only one that is

My belief in me

When the lights went out

Air forced from my lungs

And I still have

Life

Breathe

Inner strength and peace

Sitting in my soul

Limitations don't exist

Everything cums with a tongue twist

Can I have what stirs in my soul

Will fear capture my dream

Before I get to it

The fear of closing my own eyes

Can I

Forever dream

The battle with me myself and I

I am

I have been

Violated

Exploited

But I choose to live and learn

From it

Not be the violation of my life

Stand in front of the reality

That is the why who and is

Strength comes from the decision to be

Not become

Silence that was the voice of reason

screams

Confess

Pain

that travels to the brink of destruction

I write the conclusion of my imagination

That is my illusion

Turn right at my hurt

Left at the process

That releases the conviction

Stored

In your nightmares

That you gave

But I choose to return to sender

I am not the violation that you committed

I am the power that rises from the tears that once fell

Now fall for those that are still crying to be free

Deposits in my soul that become overloaded

Limitations that don't exist

Everything cums with a twist

A twist that ensures delivery of

Pure animalistic passion

Hard core desire with a spin the honey glow

To be honest with the conspiracy

That love is a telephone call away that seems

Disconnected from

Real

Life

Deposit of emotions

Sailed into nowhere

Broken Arrow keys that fail to be repaired

When you get the best

But give only for the moment

Seconds of satisfaction

Only berates the spirit of the beast that requires so much more but

it

Remains in the distance of my imagination, fighting to close in

See the light of day turns into darkness past the rise of him

When love is only temporary lust

Deposits of what should never be released

Passion lasts only for the moment unless constantly refueled if not

Deposit return to sender

Deep Rivers

I cry tears from deep within

Emotions that no longer fight

Against All Odds

I feel more than

But less than

At the same time in time, my soul cries dry

The only thing that you can utilize for the next step

Of directions that have no guidance

I walk in the darkness of sunlight

Trapped in the morning of the sun that forgot to rise

I see you far in the distance of my heart

Hidden in what was yesterday's kiss

Captured in your lack of time or time that does not exist

Love loves back

When given

But fades away when ignored

Time waits for no second or the wind to decide its direction

Nor stands still

A heartbeat that hears no sound

I am the words in the wind

Soft whistles

That only his heart will hear

If only he knew

He carries my last breath

In his lips

If

Deep Rivers

Don't judge me

Walk with me

To understand the need to be

Cravings overflow the same time

Deep Rivers and the dam breaks

You touched me

When I should have insisted you look away

My addiction takes control

Leading me to the brink of destruction

I want

Screams for

Dipped in

Master of

the Development and implementation of my imagination

See if you are looking for the first or last

The trials and tribulations that twist between the words

Of absolution

Tired of

Disgusted with

Oblivious to

A soul that whispers to be saved

Can you hear the sound

of my life?

The revival of my breath

Heart pounding that is now calm

see what looks back

the tears that fell in mid air

and landed no where at all

the consistency

the benevolent moments

words that continue to wrap me

and unfold

I cry because

yet again my heart deceived me

for a time

my heart speaks from the inside

new hardware to

revive

me

I refuse to lose this battle

I got work to do

heart attack, 2

fight to survive, priceless

and only the silent

feel me

Faulty wiring

Failed attempts at

And yet again we try

The same repetitive schedule

With heartache being the inevitable

His eyes spoke with conviction

Allowing his lips to spew deception

Once again

Warmth caresses

With constant reminders of temporary

Needing to walk away from the fantasy

Drawn into the reality

That quenches my thirst

The darkness covers the beast

That hunts his prey

A wounded flower

Craves the drop of sunlight that will

Give life

Scarred deeply

Forced to take the time to get to know me

But the fact remains

Cravings overflow the hope of emptiness

His eyes spoke to me

I cried dry tears

For the need to be filled with his heat

A touch from you

But the ship of emotions

Sailed into nowhere

Broken Heart of today

Somber moods

Lost thoughts

Emptiness all around

With emotions that have no explanation

Or direction

Intimate moments that only leave one lost

Deposit of nothing

For a temporary high

I realized that I no longer have the option

You can't continue to experience my depth

That is never to become permanent

My body went on a roller coaster high

Only to come crashing down

When it was over

You deposited your negative

Into my positive

That left me with a negative balance

And my soul has been way pass tired

Tears are dry

With a heart that whispers, why bother

The facade that surrounds us

Moments pass by

The light of day turns into darkness

When love continues to walk away

Never solidifying

Committed to nothing

With each deposit

I am left with temporary nothings

I walked in the room and quickly scanned the crowd
Broken sat in a corner all dolled up
Hurt smiles and waved
While deception stood watch as if on duty at the bank
Looked further
And who do I see
The life of the party as usual greetings to all
With a spirit of sadness that was forever present
And the sprinkles of faces that seemed just as confused as everyone else
See so many go through life with the thoughts of confusion
Or simply the hurt that has become a part of life
But the real problem is
We have so many in need of the simplest of things to the most complex
From a listening ear
A silent shoulder
To your presence with no expectations
No one really knows what someone else feels
As we are individually designed
But it doesn't take a lot just to be

I sat back and listened to the water crash against the house
Wondering if the storm would ever let up
And at this moment the odds weren't in my favor
The constant stream wont allow the silence in my head to scream
See I look around and so much devastation is smothering the air
from each individual soul
Lives lost
Freedom not found
And they keep uttering make America Great again
How when the cycle never ends
Racism is
And always has been
So how do you make it great again
Will there ever be a time that we can live together in a land of
love, respect and morality?
Not as long as they continue to water hate
Allowing hate to overdose the souls of the innocent
The rain continues
Teardrops from the skies that wash away our sins or cleanse the
soul
Whichever you choose
It would have to rain forever to relieve us of the hate
And allow unity to bloom
The curse we live that was never meant to allow us to be free
My mind screams as it no longer is my escape

From the hell we call

Earth

I have to admit
the ability to peel the layers
reveal the truth
of what is to be
what was...is
what is...ain't
what would...should
what could....never touched the surface
see the ability to reveal the truth
that lies beneath the reality
that your truth and mine
is the reverse of a just cause
slowly distorted for the picture
when the book was written
with the blood and tears
of justification
without verification
lost in the words of realization
see when you fall in love
you slowly slip into
the passion of danger
never looking for safety
because the intensity
that he brings
gives

the orgasmic smile

from the inside out

My words explode from inside
Cravings that build
Wants and desires that spill onto
A canvas of erotica
Mind filled with fantasy
Words that stroke me into yet another
World of necessity
To fuel my addiction
Your words entice me
I close my eyes and feel your caress
Your lips tour my frame
And your hands sculpt the path
That you will go
Closed eyes
See
With an open mind
Heart filled with passion
To paint life new
My words explode from the inside
With you deep in me
And then I realize
Eyes open
That I am afraid of my
Own words…..

" life of an addict"

The box that has kept me from me
cement structure that holds the tales of my darkness
raped, molested and abused but the smile that appears
never tells the secrets that never releases the light, but you did
you came into my life and started stripping away
what was put there by others not self, but you held
on strong to the darkness and I chipped away
see the ink fueled the pen and the pen beat away at the paper
writing a new beginning to the ending of the hurt and turmoil
that you went through, experienced and lived through
see the once little girl that thought she was thrown out with the
trash
poetry saved her life, one pen stroke, one key stroke, one stone
broke
one voice at a time

Lay your hand upon my skin

Feel the heat that escapes

The pain that craves you

The pain that temporarily gives me hope

Nothing against my skin

Will alleviate the pain

That runs from head to toe

Nothing releases me from the pain

I

See

Hear and close my eyes to

And it still exists

My pain greater than any thing you can ever

Imagine

When pains controls life

I am

I will

Continue

My purpose His plan.....

I cursed my soul

You sat back and allowed the constant grief to enter

Slapped the image that falls over and over again

See I try hard to understand

To rationalize the ability to continue

The reasons why I love life

Love given

And nothing

Ever comes back in return

My heart shelled in ice

Fighting to release

Fire that rages

While my emotions suffocate themselves

I cursed my soul

Body on fire

Mind is disarray

With a fight that is slowly losing

Its race

See no matter what I continue to go against what I know is the

End of my story

Love fell into the pit of hell

While lust sat back and laughed at what will never be

I am

Who"

I no longer know

Numb to reality

Stuck in a fantasy

With an image stuck in my mind

Happiness that seems to walk sideways

In my world

I let love control what I want the most

To be loved in returned…..

Staring in the mirror and death stares back...the remnants of strife...instead of the glow that once was....pushing forward as the only option I have...is in front of me....not behind...leaving the scars to only be reminders...knowing the structure of what a true relationship is....the man that provides....to give the tears of joy....to flow from these eyes...
protecting his home...his determination to have stability....when I am weak....a listening ear....just to hear me breath....and as I stand next to his side....he is my strength....I'm his soft side...I have his back through it all.....the man of his house...the final call....hand in hand...side by side....the battlefield....fought with the both of us...he is never alone...or am I....protecting his own....the battle to get back to a true family....God, man, wife and family...the order in which we may go.....without it....we will continue to have a disruptive flow.....

As I write this I can never find the words to express the thank you's that are do the people who are always there. I appreciate it from deep within as without the support this would be a struggle. I value each person that has ever taken the time to read my thoughts.

Dawn Renee

Cover design by
Steven Lester

Photo by
Kay Joe Unscripted
unscriptedforreal@gmail.com

Contact information :
Dawn Blanchard
deeprivers67@yahoo.com
Facebook
Dawn Blanchard
317-909-3188

www.ingramcontent.com/pod-product-compliance
Lightning Source LLC
Chambersburg PA
CBHW021446080526
44588CB00009B/711